Indiana

by the Capstone Press
Geography Department

Reading Consultant:
Jeff Barnett
Indianapolis Chamber of Commerce

CAPSTONE PRESS
MANKATO, MINNESOTA

C A P S T O N E   P R E S S

818 North Willow Street • Mankato, Minnesota 56001

Printed in the United States of America.

Library of Congress Cataloging-in-Publication Data
    Indiana/by the Capstone Press Geography Department
    p. cm.--(One Nation)
    Includes bibliographical references and index.
    Summary: Gives an overview of the state of Indiana, including its
history, geography, people, and living conditions.
    ISBN 1-56065-474-0
    1. Indiana--Juvenile literature. [1. Indiana.]
    I. Capstone Press. Geography Dept. II. Series.
F526.3 I53 1997
977.2--dc21

                                                    96-46854
                                                      CIP
                                                       AC

Photo credits
Daybreak Photography, cover
Flag Research Center, 4 (left)
FPG, 25, 27; Larry West, 4 (right); Peter Gridley, 5 (left);
    Jon Eisberg, 6; Frank Cezus, 21
Unicorn/Martha McBride, 5 (right)
James P. Rowan, 8, 12, 22, 28
Faith Uridel, 10, 32
Visuals Unlimited/Mark Gibson, 16
Root Resources/MacDonald, 18; J. H. Boulet Jr., 30
Gary Alan Nelson, 34

Table of Contents

Fast Facts about Indiana

State Flag

Location: In the Great Lakes region of the midwestern United States

Size: 36,420 square miles (94,692 square kilometers)

Population: 5,712,799 (1993 United States Census Bureau figures)

Capital: Indianapolis

Date admitted to the Union: December 11, 1816; the 19th state

Cardinal

Peony

Largest cities: Indianapolis, Fort Wayne, Evansville, Gary, South Bend, Hammond, Muncie, Bloomington, Anderson, Terre Haute
Nickname: The Hoosier State

State bird: Cardinal
State flower: Peony
State tree: Tulip tree
State song: *"On the Banks of the Wabash, Far Away"* by Paul Dresser

Tulip tree

Chapter 1
The Indianapolis 500

The Indianapolis 500 (Indy 500) takes place the Sunday before Memorial Day every year. Thirty-three high-speed cars race around the oval track of the Indianapolis Motor Speedway. The first to finish the 500-mile (800-kilometer) race wins. Not all drivers complete the 200 laps.

Indy 500 History
The first Indy 500 was held in 1911. Ray Harroun won that race. It took him six hours. Harroun's average speed was 74.59 miles (119.34 kilometers) per hour.

High-speed cars race the Indy 500 every year.

The West Union Bridge in Parke County was built in 1876.

Today the track record for average speed is 185.981 miles (297.570 kilometers) per hour. Arie Luyendyk set that in 1990. Some drivers reach 225 miles (360 kilometers) an hour on the straightaways. The straightaways are the straight part of the oval track.

The Indy 500 is Indiana's biggest event. More than 400,000 fans pack the Speedway's stands. No other race is held at the Speedway.

A Great Sports State

People from Indiana are called Hoosiers. They take their basketball seriously. They follow their favorite high-school teams. The state's best teams play in the state tournament. The movie *Hoosiers* was based on the 1954 state champion team.

College sports are important, too. Indiana University has won five NCAA basketball championships. Bobby Knight coached three of those teams. Notre Dame University in South Bend has a long history of having winning football teams.

The Crossroads of America

Hoosiers call their state the Crossroads of America. Interstate highways crisscross Indiana. People from all parts of the country come to Indiana.

Hoosiers and visitors enjoy outdoor fun. Lake Michigan offers swimming and boating. Wyandotte Cave has 35 miles (56 kilometers) of passages to explore. Hiking trails wind through Hoosier National Forest. More than 30 covered bridges dot Parke County.

Chapter 2

The Land

Indiana is in the Midwest. It is the smallest midwestern state. Three other midwestern states border Indiana. Ohio lies to the east. Michigan is to the north. Illinois is to the west.

The Ohio River forms Indiana's southern border. Kentucky lies across the river. Lake Michigan touches Indiana's northwestern corner.

Plains cover most of Indiana. Large sheets of ice called glaciers flattened the land. This happened thousands of years ago. The glaciers did not touch south-central Indiana. There steep hills reach up from the land.

Indiana's plains provide good farming land.

Sand dunes line Indiana's Lake Michigan shores.

The Great Lakes Plain

The Great Lakes Plain covers far northern Indiana. Hills of sand called dunes line Indiana's Lake Michigan shore. Rich farmland lies in the southern part of the state.

The Kankakee River runs west across the plain. To the east are many large lakes. Lake Wawasee is one of them. It is Indiana's largest natural lake.

The Till Plains

The Till Plains cover most of the rest of Indiana. The glaciers left rich soil there. Wheat, corn, and oats grow well. Dairy and beef cattle graze on grasses.

Indiana's highest point is on the Till Plains. It is on the Ohio border in Wayne County. The land there reaches 1,257 feet (377 meters) above sea level.

The Wabash and White rivers flow through the Till Plains. Indianapolis is on the White River.

The Wabash River flows through Lafayette and Terre Haute. Then the Wabash River forms Indiana's border with Illinois.

Southern Hills and Lowlands

Southern Indiana is the hilliest part of the state. Yet the state's lowest point is there. It is located where the Wabash River empties into the Ohio River. That land is 320 feet (96 meters) above sea level.

Hundreds of streams are in southern Indiana. They have cut narrow valleys in the hills.

Some streams flow underground. Over time, they formed large caves. Marengo Cave and Wyandotte Cave are two of them.

Coal and oil lie underground in the southwestern part of the state. Limestone is found to the east.

Climate

Indiana enjoys long, warm summers. It is warmest in the Southern Hills. Temperatures there reach more than 90 degrees Fahrenheit (32 degrees Celsius). In the north, Lake Michigan keeps the area somewhat cooler.

In the winter, the lake warms the nearby land. But, Indiana winters are still cold. Strong winds blow off Lake Michigan. They bring heavy snowfalls to northwestern Indiana.

Southern Indiana receives the most rainfall. The Ohio and other rivers often flood. Tornadoes sometimes occur in spring and summer.

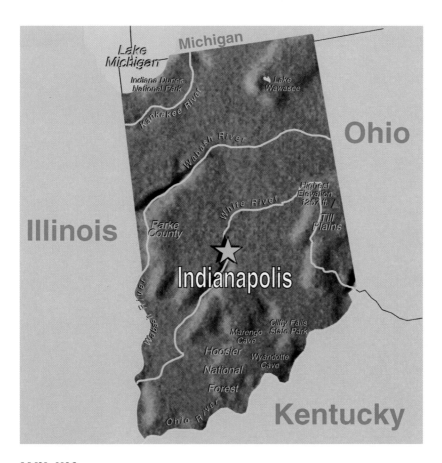

Wildlife

Raccoons, foxes, and white-tailed deer are found throughout Indiana. Coyotes live in the northeast. Quail and wild turkeys are there, too. Bass and pike swim in Indiana's lakes and rivers.

Chapter 3

The People

Indiana's nickname is the Hoosier State. Indianans call themselves Hoosiers. Many stories try to explain how this name started.

Some people believe Samuel Hoosier started the name. In 1825, he was building a canal in Kentucky. Hoosier hired workers from Indiana. They were called Hoosier's men.

Quite a few Hoosiers live in Indiana today. The state's population ranks 14th in the nation. Between 1990 and 1994, Indiana gained 200,000 Hoosiers.

Many people live in Indiana. The state's population ranks 14th in the nation.

Many Amish people live in Indiana. They lead simple lives without cars, telephones, or electricity.

Two-thirds of Hoosiers live near cities. Indianapolis is the nation's 13th largest city. Fort Wayne ranks 99th.

About 95 percent of Hoosiers were born in Indiana. Almost 91 percent of them have European backgrounds. Long ago, their families immigrated from Europe. To immigrate means to come to another country to settle.

Settlers

Farmers settled Indiana. They arrived in the late 1700s and early 1800s. Many of their ancestors were English, Irish, and German.

Settlers came from North Carolina, Virginia, and Kentucky. Later New Englanders and New Yorkers joined them. Settlers also came from neighboring Ohio.

Amish people arrived from Pennsylvania in the 1840s. They settled in northern Indiana. Many of the Amish still live simple lives in Indiana. They drive horse-drawn buggies. They work their fields with horse-drawn plows. Their homes have no telephones or electricity.

European Immigrants

Some Indiana people came directly from Europe. French people settled Vincennes in the 1730s. About 2,500 Swiss founded Vevay in 1801. Irish workers came in the 1830s. They helped build the Wabash and Erie Canal. English and German farmers came, too.

Between 1880 and 1920, Eastern European immigrants arrived. Many came from Poland,

Greece, and Italy. Some worked in southwestern Indiana's coal mines. Others found jobs in northwestern steel mills.

African Americans

Slavery was never legal in Indiana. By 1860, about 11,500 free African Americans lived in the state.

After the Civil War (1861-1865), slavery ended in the South. Some newly freed African Americans moved to Indiana.

During the early 1900s, more African Americans moved to Indiana. They found jobs in shops and factories. Many worked in Gary's steel mills.

Today 8 percent of Hoosiers are African American. Most of them live in Gary and Indianapolis.

Native Americans

The word Indiana means Land of the Indians. Only about 12,500 Native Americans live there today. White settlement pushed them west in the 1800s.

In the 1900s, many moved to work in Indiana's steel mills.

Other Ethnic Groups

About 2 percent of Indiana's population is Hispanic. Their families speak Spanish or have Spanish-speaking backgrounds. Most of them are from Mexico. Others have come from Puerto Rico and Cuba.

Few Asian Americans live in Indiana. The number is growing, however. Most of them came from China, India, and Korea.

Chapter 4

Indiana History

Indiana's first people arrived about 10,000 years ago. Later, people called mound builders lived there. They built huge dirt mounds. Some mounds still stand in the Ohio Valley.

Native Americans moved into Indiana in the 1600s and 1700s. They included the Shawnee, Miami, Delaware, and Potawatomi tribes.

The French Arrive

In the 1600s, France claimed land in the Ohio Valley. Indiana was in the middle of it.

Robert Cavelier, sieur de La Salle, came from Canada in 1679. He was the first European to see Indiana.

In the 1600s, Indiana was in the middle of the French-claimed land of the Ohio Valley.

French fur traders followed La Salle. They traded with Native Americans for furs. The French built trading posts and forts.

Indiana Becomes English

By 1732, England had 13 colonies. A colony is a group of people who settle in a distant land but remain under the control of their native country. The colonies were along the Atlantic Ocean. England also claimed land in the Ohio Valley.

England and France fought for control of that land. This was called the French and Indian War (1754-1763). Native Americans helped the French.

England won the war. France lost its land east of the Mississippi River. English soldiers took over Indiana's French forts.

The Revolutionary War

In 1775, the 13 colonies rebelled against England. This started the Revolutionary War (1775-1783). The colonies became the United States of America.

The French lost Indiana's land to England in the French and Indian War (1754-1763).

George Rogers Clark led American troops into Indiana. The United States claimed the land when troops captured Vincennes in 1779.

The war ended in 1783. The United States gained England's land, including Indiana.

Part of America

By 1800, about 5,000 Americans lived in Indiana. Several Native American tribes lived there, too. The Native Americans joined together. They tried to save their land from the settlers.

United States troops defeated the Native Americans at the Battle of Tippecanoe in 1811. Many Native Americans left Indiana. By 1815, European settlers had claimed all the Native American land in Indiana.

In 1816, Indiana became the 19th state. Eight years later, Indianapolis became the state capital.

The New State

Indiana's population continued to grow. Settlers followed the National Road into the state. This road ran across the middle of Indiana.

Later, railroads linked Indiana to the East Coast. The railroads allowed Indiana's farmers to ship their crops out of the state.

In the 1850s, factories opened. The Studebaker brothers started a wagon shop in South Bend. The Gatling gun was made in Indianapolis in 1862.

Hoosiers helped the North win the Civil War (1861-1865). Soldiers ate canned pork and beans. They came from Indianapolis' Van Camp Company.

George Rogers Clark helped claim Indiana during the Revolutionary War (1775-1783).

In Indiana, the number of people without jobs is low. Some Hoosiers are employed at the Fort Wayne Children's Zoo.

Mining and Industry

After the war, mining became a big Indiana business. Terre Haute was a coal-mining center. A natural gas well opened in Portland in 1886. Indiana's first oil well was drilled in 1889 near Keystone.

New companies moved to Indiana. In 1889, Standard Oil built a large refinery in Whiting. It made gasoline from oil. Nearby, United States Steel founded the city of Gary. It built a huge steel mill there. Other companies started building cars.

World Wars and Depression

Hoosiers helped the United States win World War I (1914-1918). They made steel and grew food crops.

The Great Depression (1929-1939) hurt the nation. By 1932, one-fourth of Hoosier workers had lost their jobs. The steel mills had slowed down. Many Indiana farmers lost their land.

The United States entered World War II (1939-1945) in 1941. Hoosiers made medicines for the troops. They also made bombs and airplane engines.

Changes Come to Indiana

After the war, Indiana's cities became crowded. A large number of families moved to the suburbs. A suburb is a town close to a big city. Some businesses also left the cities. Others laid off many workers.

By the mid-1990s, Hoosiers were doing better. The number of people without jobs was fairly low. Indiana's government was working hard. It helped bring new businesses to the state. Still, some companies continued to lay off workers.

Chapter 5
Indiana Business

Taken together, service industries employ the most Hoosiers. Trade and tourism are important service businesses. Banking and government are other service businesses.

Manufacturing is Indiana's single-largest business. Mining and farming are important Indiana businesses, too.

Manufacturing
Indiana leads the states in making steel. Gary has one of the world's biggest mills. This is the United States Steel plant. Indiana's steel is shipped all over the world.

Indiana leads all other states in making steel.

Farmers throughout Indiana grow corn and other crops.

Some of the steel stays in Indiana. Hoosiers use it to make cars and trucks.

Factories in Indianapolis, Evansville, and Elkhart make medicines. Other factories make soap. Hoosiers also make telephone and television equipment.

Agriculture

Farmers throughout Indiana grow corn and soybeans. Hay and wheat are other important Indiana grains.

Tomatoes are Indiana's leading vegetable crop. Potatoes and cucumbers are other important vegetables. Fruit crops include apples and peaches.

Hogs are Indiana's leading livestock. Indiana's farmers also raise dairy cattle and chickens. Only California produces more eggs than Indiana.

Hoosiers also raise greenhouse plants. Their tulip bulbs are sold throughout the country.

Mining

Indiana is a leading coal-mining state. Coal is Indiana's largest mining product. Most of it comes from southwestern Indiana.

Indiana also has large deposits of limestone. Buildings can be made with blocks of limestone. Crushed limestone is used to make roads.

Oil is another important Indiana mining product. Southwestern Indiana has a large amount of oil.

Service Industries

Tourism brings several billion dollars to Indiana each year. Travelers spend this money at hotels, restaurants, and resorts.

Government is another important Indiana service. Public school teachers are some Hoosier government workers.

Chapter 6

Seeing the Sights

Seeing the sights is easy in Indiana. Many highways crisscross the state. They take travelers to big cities and small towns. They also reach state parks and a national lakeshore.

Northern Indiana

Gary is in far northwestern Indiana. Michael Jackson was born there. Fans stop to see the house where he grew up.

Gary is also close to Illinois. Some people in Gary work in Illinois. Many Illinoisans visit Gary's riverboat casinos. A casino is a place to gamble. The boats sit in a harbor off Lake Michigan.

Abraham Lincoln's cabin is one of Indiana's sights to see.

East of Gary is Indiana Dunes National Lakeshore. Clean, sandy beaches line Lake Michigan. Dunes rise in the background. Mount Baldy is the tallest dune. It is 135 feet (41 meters) high.

South Bend is farther east. This city is the home of the University of Notre Dame. About 10,000 students attend classes there. The Fighting Irish sports teams have fans around the country.

Nappanee is southeast of South Bend. Many Amish farms are outside of town. Amish Acres is a restored farm. Visitors can enjoy Amish cooking there. They can also take a horse-drawn buggy ride.

Fort Wayne is to the southeast of Nappanee. This is Indiana's second-largest city. General "Mad Anthony" Wayne built a fort there in 1794. Today, the fort has been rebuilt. Costumed guides describe life in the 1700s.

Indianapolis

Indianapolis lies in the middle of the state. This is Indiana's largest city. It is also the state capital. The capitol building is made of Indiana limestone.

Nearby is the Soldiers and Sailors Monument. It is 284 feet (85 meters) high. Inside visitors can climb stairs to the top.

Indianapolis is a big sports town. Market Square Arena draws basketball fans. They watch the Indiana Pacers shoot hoops. The RCA Dome is home to the Indianapolis Colts. They play football there.

The Indianapolis Motor Speedway is north of downtown. Every year the Indy 500 is held there. Visitors can take a bus trip around the track. Next to the track is the Hall of Fame Museum. It displays many winning Indy cars.

Other Central Indiana Sights

Muncie is south of Fort Wayne. It is the home of the Ball Corporation headquarters. This company makes Ball jars. Food is preserved in them.

Ball State University is in Muncie. This school is named for the Ball family. David Letterman is one of its graduates.

West Lafayette is west of Muncie. It is home to Purdue University. More than 15 astronauts graduated from this school. They include Gus Grissom and Frank Borman.

Rockville is south of Lafayette. Historic Billie Creek Village is there. This is an 1890s working farm. Three covered bridges are on the grounds.

Bloomington lies to the southeast of Rockville. Indiana University is there. Almost 35,000 students attend. Its art museums and concerts are open to the public.

Southern Indiana

Clifty Falls State Park is in southeastern Indiana. It overlooks the Ohio River. Big Clifty Falls drops 70 feet (21 meters). The falls ends in Clifty Creek.

French Lick is southwest of the falls. It was known for its mineral springs. Now it is known as basketball player Larry Bird's hometown. Travelers come year-round to French Lick's resorts. They play golf and tennis in the summer. They ski and ice skate in the winter.

West of the Hoosier National Forest is the Lincoln Boyhood National Memorial. This

marks the spot where Abraham Lincoln, the 16th president of the United States, grew up.

East of the Memorial lies the little town of Santa Claus. Stacks of mail come to its post office each December. People want their Christmas cards postmarked from Santa Claus.

Indiana Time Line

8000 B.C.—First people live in Indiana.

A. D. 1679—Robert Cavelier, sieur de La Salle, explores Indiana for France.

1732—The French build a fort near Vincennes.

1763—Indiana becomes part of England's North American lands.

1779—During the Revolutionary War, George Rogers Clark's forces capture Vincennes.

1811—William Henry Harrison defeats the Shawnee at the Battle of Tippecanoe.

1816—Indiana becomes the 19th state.

1825—Indianapolis becomes the state capital.

1842—The University of Notre Dame is founded in South Bend.

1889—Indiana Senator Benjamin Harrison becomes the 23rd president of the United States; Standard Oil builds Indiana's first oil refinery.

1906—U.S. Steel Company founds the city of Gary.

1911—The first Indy 500 race takes place.

1967—Richard D. Hatcher is elected mayor of Gary and becomes one of the first two African-American mayors of a large American city.

1970—The governments of Marion County and Indianapolis are united.

1984—The Hoosier Dome opens and the Colts football team moves to Indianapolis.

1987—Indiana University wins its third NCAA basketball championship since 1976.

1989—Indiana native Dan Quayle becomes vice president of the United States under George Bush.

1990—Driver Arie Luyendyk sets an Indy 500 average speed record of 185.981 miles (297.570 kilometers) per hour.

1996—Scott King becomes Gary's first white mayor since 1967; the bones of a mastodon are unearthed in an Indiana backyard.

Famous Hoosiers

Adelle Davis (1904-1974) Nutritionist who wrote books encouraging people to become healthy by eating natural foods; born in Lizton.

Jim Davis (1945-) Creator of the Garfield comic strip.

James Dean (1931-1955) Movie actor who starred in *Rebel Without a Cause*, *Giant*, and *East of Eden*; born in Marion.

Eugene V. Debs (1855-1926) Labor leader who ran for president five times as a socialist candidate; born in Terre Haute.

Theodore Dresier (1871-1945) Novelist who wrote *Sister Carrie* and other works about American society; born in Terre Haute.

Benjamin Harrison (1833-1901) Politician who served as U.S. senator from Indiana (1881-1887) and as U.S. president (1889-1893).

Michael Jackson (1958-) Singer, dancer, and songwriter; born in Gary.

David Letterman (1947-) Comedian who hosts a late-night talk show; born in Indianapolis.

Carole Lombard (1909-1941) Actress who played comedy roles in such movies as *My Man Godfrey*; born in Fort Wayne.

Jane Pauley (1950-) Television journalist who co-hosted *The Today Show* and now hosts *Dateline*; born in Indianapolis.

Dan Quayle (1947-) Politician who served as vice president of the United States (1989-1993); born in Indianapolis.

Oscar Robertson (1938-) Hall of Fame basketball guard who set many scoring records; played high-school basketball in Indianapolis.

Twyla Tharp (1941-) Dancer and choreographer who creates dances for the stage and movies; born in Portland.

Madame C. J. Walker (1867-1919) Built a perfume and cosmetics factory in Indianapolis; became the first African-American woman millionaire.

Words to Know

ancestor—a person from whom one is descended

astronaut—a person who travels in and studies outer space

casino—a place where gambling takes place

colony—a group of people who settle in a distant land but remain under the control of their native country

dune—a sand hill that lines a beach or rises in a desert

glacier—a huge sheet of slowly moving ice

immigrate—to come to another country to settle.

manufacturing—the making of products

population—the number of people living in a place

suburb—a smaller town close to a big city

tornado—a powerful windstorm that comes with a whirling, funnel-shaped cloud

tourism—the business of providing services such as lodging and food for travelers

To Learn More

Aylesworth, Thomas G. and Virginia L. Aylesworth. *Eastern Great Lakes*. New York: Chelsea House, 1991.

Berry, S. L. *Indianapolis*. A Downtown America Book. Minneapolis: Dillion Press, 1990.

Blashfield, Jean F. and Nancy Jacobson. *Awesome Almanac: Indiana*. Fontana, Wis.: B & B Publishing, 1993.

Fradin, Dennis B. *Indiana*. Sea to Shining Sea. Chicago: Children's Press, 1994.

Thompson, Kathleen. *Indiana*. Portrait of America. Austin, Tex.: Raintree Steck-Vaughn Publishers, 1996.

Useful Addresses

Amish Acres
1600 West Market Street
Nappanee, IN 46550

Covered Bridge Country Visitor Bureau
2 South Jackson Street
Greencastle, IN 46135

Indiana Dunes National Lakeshore
1100 North Mineral Springs Road
Porter, IN 46304

Indianapolis Motor Speedway Hall of Fame Museum
4790 West 16th Street
Indianapolis, IN 46222

Madame Walker Urban Life Center and Theatre
617 Indiana Avenue
Indianapolis, IN 46202

Squire Boone Caverns and Village
P.O. Box 411
Corydon, IN 47112

Internet Sites

City.Net Indiana
http://city.net/countries/united_states/indiana

Travel.org—Indiana
http://travel.org/indiana.html

Indiana Information Network
http://www.state.in.us

The Auto Channel—Indy 500 News
http://www.theautochannel.com/news/events/
indy500/indynews.html

Index